WILMA MANKILLER

Chief of the Cherokee Nation

by
Bruce Glassman

A BLACKBIRCH PRESS™ BOOK

THE ROSEN PUBLISHING GROUP, INC.

Published by Blackbirch Press™ in conjunction with The Rosen
Publishing Group, Inc., 29 East 21st Street, New York, NY 10010

©1992 Blackbirch Press™ a division of Blackbirch Graphics, Inc.
First Edition

Printed in Hong Kong
Bound in the United States of America

Editors: Kailyard Associates

Library of Congress Cataloging-in-Publication Data

Glassman, Bruce.
    Wilma Mankiller: chief of the Cherokee nation / Bruce Glassman.
—1st ed.
    (The Library of famous women)
    "A Blackbirch Press book."
    Includes bibliographical references and index.
    Summary: Discusses the life and career of the first female to be
chief of the Cherokee Nation.
    ISBN 0-8239-1208-6
    1. Mankiller, Wilma P., 1945– —Juvenile literature. 2. Cherokee
Indians—Biography—Juvenile literature. 3. Cherokee Indians—Kings
and rulers—Juvenile literature. [1. Mankiller, Wilma P., 1945– .
2. Cherokee Indians—Biography. 3. Indians of North America—
Biography.] I. Title. II. Series.
E99.C5M464   1991
973'.0497502—dc20
  [B]   91-28249
                                                CIP
                                                AP

Contents

Introduction

"If I had another life, I'd spend all my time just on education. I would try to impact the kind of information that Americans get every day, information about what is essentially every American's history, the history of our native people."

The official seal of the Cherokee Nation

When most people hear the word "Indian," they get a very specific picture in their minds. Most people think of a tall man with stripes painted on his face, wearing a headdress, sitting on a horse, and saying "How." But this kind of Indian does not really exist. Hollywood moviemakers made up what they *thought* Indians were like. If you have never met a real Native American, you may have only a movie image in your head.

Though they have a distinct culture, real Native Americans look, act, and speak much like other Americans. They live in cities and in the country. Some work in big offices, others work on farms. Like other ethnic groups in the United States, most

(Opposite page)
Wilma presides over a meeting about rivers and water in her region.

5

The headquarters of the Cherokee Nation is located in Tahlequah, Oklahoma.

Indians have blended their own special culture with the culture of mainstream America.

Native American Life

Unlike other ethnic groups, Native Americans play a very special role in American history. They were the first people to settle in North America. Their past is both painful and magnificent. And their culture is rich in tradition and wisdom. Despite this, very few non-Indians know much about Native Americans. But now there are people who are working to teach non-Indians about Native American life—past and present. One person who is working hard to show others what Indian life is really like is Wilma Mankiller.

Only a small group of people know about this woman. Yet, to those that know her—or know of her—her name means a lot.

Wilma Mankiller is the principal chief of the Cherokee Nation. She is the first woman to be chief of the Cherokees. The Cherokee Nation is comprised of more than 120,000 Native Americans, the second largest U.S. tribe after the Navajos. The center of the government is located in Tahlequah, Oklahoma. There, Chief Mankiller manages a budget of $52 million a year, which includes $23 million in federal funding. Wilma Mankiller often says her job is "like running a small country." In many ways, that is true.

In addition to being the head of the Cherokees, Wilma Mankiller has dedicated herself to teaching the world about Native American culture. She has also spent much of her life helping other Native Americans improve their lives.

Becoming chief of the Cherokees was not easy. It took great dedication and a good deal of faith. But those are two things Wilma Mankiller has plenty of.

Chapter 1

Child of the Cherokee Nation

Wilma Mankiller was born in 1945, in the small Oklahoma town of Tahlequah. The hospital where she and her siblings were born still stands today. It is used as an educational center by Northeastern Oklahoma State University. History and tradition are important pieces of daily life in the area.

Tahlequah has been a longstanding meeting place for Cherokees in Oklahoma. In the 1940s, it was the center of activity for the region. "There was a tremendous Cherokee influence," Wilma says. "Street signs were in Cherokee and English; there was a lot more Cherokee spoken at public functions and at gatherings. And it was much more common to run into someone who was monolingual—who only spoke one language: Cherokee. Nowadays, you very rarely run into anyone who can't speak English."

(Opposite page)
Wilma feels a very strong tie to her Cherokee heritage and has learned much from the community's elders.

The only modern transportation available to Tahlequah citizens in 1940 was a train that stopped in town. That was how people traveled long distances. Roads were in poor shape and most towns in the area were isolated from one another. Cars were not common, and when someone went visiting to another town, they went for days, not hours.

Today, Tahlequah is the capital of the Cherokee Nation. A large strip of highway runs through the center of town. Department stores and fast-food restaurants share the roadside with Cherokee-owned businesses, the Cherokee Heritage Center, and town buildings. A modern midsized city, Tahlequah has the look of any other typical midwestern American town.

Early Beginnings

Wilma Mankiller's parents met in Stilwell, where her grandmother ran a boarding house. Wilma remembers her grandmother as "a very active and outgoing, strong lady. She knew lots of people in town and somehow, through her, my parents got together." Charlie, Wilma's father, was 100 percent Cherokee. He descended from people that lived in the Tennessee region. Wilma's mother, Irene, was Dutch-Irish. She descended from a family that had lived in Oklahoma for nearly 100 years.

There were 11 children in the Mankiller family. Wilma was a middle child, and she usually lived with nine brothers and sisters under the same roof. But the Mankiller clan was much larger than just the parents and children. Aunts, uncles, cousins, and other family were all close by. Regular visits helped to maintain a constant feeling of shared tradition and heritage. This early feeling of shared heritage would stay with Wilma for the rest of her life. The strong Cherokee culture she was given as a young girl would form an important part of her identity as an adult.

"The elders in my family told me a lot of old Cherokee stories," she remembers, "and old scary stories that they had heard from their ancestors. So that whole Cherokee culture was all-pervasive and had a great influence on my early life." Wilma says that her father and his sister (her aunt) had the greatest influence on her. It was their determination to keep Native American culture alive in their children that impressed young Wilma so much.

"The Cherokee culture had a great influence on my early life."

(Opposite page)
Some whites tried to help the Indians by urging them to fight those who were taking away tribal lands.

Life for the Cherokees when Wilma was growing up was not easy. It had not been easy since the first white man stepped foot on the land we now call North America. Since that time, Cherokees as well as other Native American tribes have been abused and neglected by the governments white Americans have put in place.

The Story of Cherokees in America

When European settlers first arrived in the New World, the Cherokees were one of the largest and most powerful tribes on the continent. Most of the tribe lived in the Great Smoky Mountain region, in what are now the states of Virginia, North and South Carolina, Georgia, Tennessee, and Alabama.

The Cherokees thrived in the fertile valleys of North America and developed many sophisticated ways of living. The tribe was divided into seven clans, with members living in every village. By the time of the American Revolution, most Cherokees had discarded their traditional rectangular homes constructed of wooden poles. Instead, they lived in log cabins similar to the ones built by European settlers.

As talented farmers and plantation owners, many Cherokees were prospering by the beginning of the nineteenth century.

In 1831, the Cherokees tried unsuccessfully to stop the state of Georgia from taking away Indian lands.

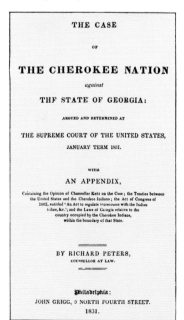

THE CASE

OF

THE CHEROKEE NATION

against

THE STATE OF GEORGIA:

ARGUED AND DETERMINED AT

THE SUPREME COURT OF THE UNITED STATES,

JANUARY TERM 1831.

WITH

AN APPENDIX,

Containing the Opinion of Chancellor Kent on the Case ; the Treaties between the United States and the Cherokee Indians ; the Act of Congress of 1802, entitled ' An Act to regulate intercourse with the Indian tribes, &c.'; and the Laws of Georgia relative to the country occupied by the Cherokee Indians, within the boundary of that State.

BY RICHARD PETERS,

COUNSELLOR AT LAW.

Philadelphia:

JOHN GRIGG, 9 NORTH FOURTH STREET.

1831.

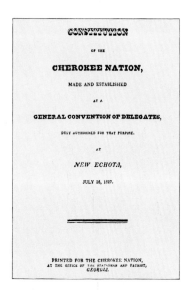

CONSTITUTION
OF THE
CHEROKEE NATION,
MADE AND ESTABLISHED
AT A
GENERAL CONVENTION OF DELEGATES,
DULY AUTHORIZED FOR THAT PURPOSE.
AT
NEW ECHOTA,
JULY 26, 1827.

PRINTED FOR THE CHEROKEE NATION,
AT THE OFFICE OF THE STATESMAN AND PATRIOT,
GEORGIA.

The Treaty of New Echota took Cherokee lands and gave them to white settlers.

(Opposite page)
In the 1830s, some Native Americans tried to cooperate with the U.S. government. They soon found out that government promises were often not kept.

In 1821, a mixed-blood Cherokee named Sequoya, developed a Cherokee alphabet. Within a few years, this alphabet was used to create native Cherokee literature. The written tradition of the Cherokees remains to this day, an important part of their daily culture.

As white people continued to push westward, the Cherokee lifestyle and home became more threatened. The advance of white civilization prompted the Cherokees to organize into one unified tribal state, with special offices held by priests, warriors, and elders. This new tribal state was concerned with containing the growing hatred and violence between the Cherokees and European settlers.

In 1828, gold was discovered in Cherokee country. Soon, pressure from whites forced the removal of the Cherokees from their traditional lands. The state of Georgia forced the Indians to leave. In 1831, the Cherokees petitioned the U.S. Supreme Court, hoping to stop the violence and destruction to their society. The Supreme Court said the Cherokees had no real right to the Smoky Mountain region, only the right of occupancy. But occupancy was becoming harder and harder. Continued

pressure on the tribe caused a handful of
Cherokees to sign the Treaty of New
Echota. This treaty—written entirely by the
U.S. government—gave all Cherokee lands
over to whites.

The Creator of the Cherokee Written Language

Sequoya was a Cherokee of mixed ancestry. In fact, he had two names. Sequoya was his Cherokee name, but he sometimes went by the name George Guess. Sequoya is known as the inventor of the Cherokee written language.

As a young man, Sequoya was a respected hunter, warrior, trader, and craftsperson. He specialized in working with silver. Sequoya was also a very talented speaker. He spoke French, Spanish, and English in addition to his native Cherokee.

Sequoya was fiercely proud of his Cherokee heritage. And he became very angry when he saw whites intruding on Indian culture and lands. Sequoya also recognized the power of the written word. By the time he was about 40 years old, he had created a special series of written symbols. Each symbol was adapted from a character in English, but each represented a special sound in the Cherokee language.

By the early 1800s, Sequoya's language was being used. The new Cherokee written language made it possible for a Cherokee newspaper to be created. The *Cherokee Phoenix*, the first Cherokee language newspaper, was founded on February 21, 1828.

Sequoya

Cherokee Alphabet.

D a	**R** e	**T** i	Ꮄ o	**O** u	**i** v
S ga Ꭷ ka	**F** ge	**y** gi	**A** go	**J** gu	**E** gv
Ꮦ ha	**P** he	**Ꭿ** hi	**F** ho	**Γ** hu	**Ꮗ** hv
W la	**Ꮭ** le	**P** li	**G** lo	**M** lu	**Ꭾ** lv
Ꮌ ma	**Ꭴ** me	**H** mi	**Ꮋ** mo	**y** mu	
Ꮎ na **Ꮗ** hna **G** nah	**Λ** ne	**h** ni	**Z** no	**Ꮙ** nu	**O** nv
T qua	**Ꮚ** que	**Ꮔ** qui	**V** quo	**Ꮞ** quu	**Ɛ** quv
U sa **Ꭷ** s	**4** se	**b** si	**Ʇ** so	**Ꮞ** su	**R** sv
Ꮮ da **W** ta	**Ꮥ** de **Ꮦ** te	**Ꮲ** di **Ꮏ** ti	**V** do	**S** du	**Ꮕ** dv
Ꮐ dla **Ꮭ** tla	**L** tle	**C** tli	**Ꮪ** tlo	**Ꮱ** tlu	**P** tlv
Ꮳ tsa	**V** tse	**Ir** tsi	**K** tso	**J** tsu	**Ꮶ** tsv
G wa	**Ᏻ** we	**Ꭴ** wi	**Ꮼ** wo	**Ꮢ** wu	**6** wv
Ꮹ ya	**B** ye	**Ꭻ** yi	**Ꭽ** yo	**Ꮽ** yu	**B** yv

17

The Journey to Oklahoma

By the late 1820's, 7,000 U.S. Army troops arrived to enforce the fraudulent Treaty of Echota. About 14,000 Cherokees were to be sent to the Cherokee Indian Territory, in what is now the state of Oklahoma. In a matter of days, they were forced to pack their belongings and leave the land that had been their home for centuries. Their journey to Oklahoma is commonly known as the "Trail of Tears" because of the harsh conditions that were faced on the trip. More than 4,000 Cherokees died of exhaustion and cold along the way.

Since that time, some of the land in the Smoky Mountains has been regained by Cherokee tribes and protected by law. But the largest concentration of Cherokees now reside in Oklahoma. The Cherokee people have spent much of the twentieth century rebuilding the culture that was destroyed by the whites. The price of the Trail of Tears and the destruction of the Cherokee social systems is still not fully known. Still, the Cherokees remain unified. They are determined to improve their lives no matter where they are or what problems they have faced.

The "Trail of Tears"

By 1820, many Native American tribes had lived in close contact with white settlers for almost 100 years. The largest tribes were the Cherokee, Chickasaw, Choctaw, Creek, and Seminole. These five tribes lived mainly in the southeastern part of the continent—in what are now the states of Georgia, Tennessee, Virginia, and others. To the whites, these tribes were known as the "Five Civilized Tribes." The whites called them that because many of the Indians had adopted habits and customs of the white settlers. Of course, the Native Americans had been civilized long before the white settlers ever arrived on the shores.

During this time in the early 1800s, the population of settlers grew very fast. As their numbers grew, they wanted more and more land to call their own. Soon, the U.S. government began taking land away from the Indians so whites could settle. By 1819, the government was pushing the southeastern tribes to move west. They wanted the Indians to move to the wild and unsettled areas of Oklahoma. In 1824, the United States built two forts in Oklahoma. They were called Fort Gibson and Fort Towson. Once the forts were

The "Trail of Tears" began in Chattanooga, Tennessee, and ended at Fort Gibson, in Oklahoma.

The "Trail of Tears"
October, 1838

(Continued from page 19)

finished, the U.S. government began to force Native Americans to leave their lands in order to move west.

Between 1820 and 1842, long, sad lines of Indians moved across the wooded hills and open grasslands of Tennessee, Georgia, and other areas. Most Indians were made to walk the entire distance

to Oklahoma. The route they took is known today as the "Trail of Tears." It was given that name by the Indians who suffered the terrible trip. With little food and harsh weather, many Indians died. Of the people who survived the journey, many were very sick.

When the Indians arrived in Oklahoma, they were given the rights to nearly all of the state. Each of the five major tribes formed a nation. And each nation was given a designated area. The Cherokees took the northeastern corner of the state. By treaties, the U.S. government promised to protect the Native American nations. The United States said that the Indians would own their own lands "as long as grass shall grow and rivers run."

Other than a few written promises, the U.S. government offered very little to the Native American nations in Oklahoma. For most, the first years in the new area were very hard. But after a while, the Indians built schools and churches, cleared land, and started farms. Today, the various nations—particularly the Cherokee—are growing in prosperity. In addition, they have developed strong networks for keeping their culture and heritage alive.

About 4,000 Cherokees died on the long journey to Oklahoma.

Chapter 2

The Promise of a New Life

When Wilma was 11 years old, she learned of a new program being started by the U.S. government. It was headed by the Bureau of Indian Affairs (BIA) and was aimed at improving life for Native Americans all across the country. The program moved Indian families out of their rural settings and into cities where they could find work and a higher standard of living.

"It was supposed to be a better life for us," Wilma remembers, "because life was very hard in Stilwell. Life was very hard for everyone back then in eastern Oklahoma. We didn't think we were particularly bad off because everyone we knew was in the same situation. But my father knew better, and he knew it had become increasingly difficult just to feed all of us. So the idea of moving to a city, having a regular full-time job, and a regular income seemed attractive to him." But Wilma and her brothers

(Opposite page)
Wilma moved to San Francisco, California, with her family when she was 11 years old.

The Arts and Crafts of the Eastern Woodlands Indians

The Cherokees were one of the many Native American groups that lived in the southeastern region of North America before the 1830s. Together with other area tribes, these Native Americans are called the Eastern Woodlands Indians. There were about 22 different tribes that were native to the Eastern Woodlands region. In addition to the Cherokee, the area supported the Natchez, the Shawnee, the Algonkin, and many others.

The Cherokee lived mostly in the area south of the Ohio River. Today, this region contains Tennessee, Kentucky, Georgia, and Virginia. There, the Cherokee had a rich tradition of arts and crafts. Much of their artwork showed spirits from nature. The Indians believed that animals, trees, and natural forces like rain and snow had spirits and powers. The Indians performed dances and rituals that were created to please these spirits. Their artwork, too, was meant to please the forces that controlled their world.

Craftwork was a mix of beauty and usefulness. Most crafts were made from plant and animal elements that were not used for food or shelter. Bones, feathers, and various plants were often used for decoration. Because the Eastern Woodlands Indians lived in areas that had large wooded areas, most of their crafts were made from woodlands plants and animals. Squirrels, deer, and bear were some of the most plentiful resources. Pots, feathered pipes, and jewelry were some of the most commonly made crafts. Masks and weapons were often made from wood and other materials found in the forested areas of the region.

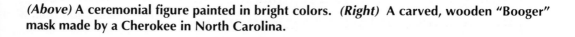

(Above) A ceremonial figure painted in bright colors. **(Right)** A carved, wooden "Booger" mask made by a Cherokee in North Carolina.

❖

"It was supposed to be a better life for us."

and sisters were not eager to leave their home. "We hated to leave, and we asked to stay with friends or cousins." Wilma's parents did not agree. In 1957, the Mankiller family left Stilwell for the big city of San Francisco, California. "We ended up getting on a train in Stilwell, leaving a home with no telephone and no indoor plumbing. We had never seen a television. We had lived in an isolated but supportive community, and we ended up living in the notorious Tenderloin district of San Francisco. It was quite a change."

There were, indeed, many problems neither the Mankillers nor the BIA had foreseen. One was adjusting to a completely new setting. For young Wilma and her family, San Francisco was so foreign that it was almost like another planet. "Both my mother and father felt sort of alienated [outcast]," Wilma remembers. The BIA had also failed to realize that moving people from their native lands, where their culture and heritage flourish, shocks a family. Living in a strange and hostile environment did not improve the Mankillers' lives. Economic opportunities were greater in the city, but many other qualities of life suffered. Worst of all, the Mankillers' identity was sacrificed.

According to Wilma, "The BIA had this philosophy then. They thought if they could take all the Indians from their tribal community and move them to an urban area, it would solve all their social problems." Charlie Mankiller and Don, Wilma's brother, found employment in an assembly plant for 40 dollars a week. Their salaries supported a wife and eight children still at home. Aching for a safer environment, Charlie moved his family to a home in a better neighborhood. But the rent soon proved to be too much, and the Mankillers wound up in a San Francisco housing project. Young Wilma doubted that life in the big city was going to be an improvement over Oklahoma.

Many of the people the Mankillers left in Oklahoma knew that city life would be filled with problems and dangers. Knowing this, few people actually relocated. The BIA program was a failure. Still, the program did have an effect on the Tahlequah community. It showed many Cherokees that leaving their homeland would not solve their problems.

Growing Up in California

Wilma spent most of her young adult years in San Francisco. She attended high school there and got married soon after graduating. She and her husband, Hector Olaya, had their first child in 1964. It was a daughter, named Felicia. In 1966, Wilma's second daughter, Gina, was born. The new family lived together in San Francisco for about nine years. In 1971, Wilma suffered the loss of her father from kidney disease. Her father's death seems to have been a turning point for Wilma. In 1972, she enrolled at San Francisco State University as a freshman. At S.F. State, Wilma studied social welfare programs. These programs provide a helping hand to poor communities. Much of the time, social welfare programs help to make physical improvements in the community. And these programs often show members of a community how to help themselves.

Wilma spent some of her college time back in Oklahoma, at an independent university, but most of her schooling was done in California. These were not easy years for Wilma, now a student and mother. By 1974, still in school, she was divorced from her first husband.

But these setbacks did not lessen Wilma's enthusiasm for her education. She knew that what she was learning would be very

valuable to her old community back in Oklahoma. And she knew that her studies could make a difference in the lives of her fellow Native Americans. Wilma's hope of helping the Cherokees gave her the will to continue studying.

Wilma enrolled at San Francisco State University in 1972.

Chapter 3

A Community Planner Finds Her Mission

In 1976, Wilma returned to her birthplace. But this first homecoming did not exactly work out. Her college degree was still unfinished, and she was unable to find work. After six months, she returned—discouraged—to California. But Wilma could not stay away for long. By 1977, she returned once again, determined to make a life in Oklahoma. In that same year, she accepted her first position working with the Cherokee Nation.

Working for the Cherokee Nation

Her first job, as Wilma puts it, was "to run around like crazy for two months" trying to enroll young Indian students in a national environmental studies program. The program was funded by the U.S. Department of Labor. Its goal was to train Native Americans in environmental science.

By 1979, Wilma had earned a Bachelor of Science degree. But her studies left her somewhat unfulfilled. As she remembers, "I felt a little bored with just putting together social programs, and I wanted to figure out how to put together an entire community." With that in mind, Wilma went on to a graduate school program at the University of Arkansas.

Soon after starting at the University of Arkansas, Wilma had a frightening brush with death. Driving home from classes one day, she collided head-on with an oncoming car. Wilma was seriously injured, but was still alive. A number of painful and complicated operations followed. The ordeal changed the way Wilma saw her life. She now speaks of the "woman who lived before and the woman who lived after."

Her time at the University of Arkansas taught Wilma much about planning improvement programs for communities. For the first time, she had the opportunity to work on designing entire communities. She had to think about what it would be like for people to actually live in the places she created. This meant that she had to understand architecture, design, and engineering. If a community needs an

Programs at the University of Arkansas taught Wilma much about planning communities.

irrigation system, for example, it needs someone to design it. That person needs to know what kinds of materials would be strong enough to do the job and how the whole system would work. And that person must figure out how equipment would get to the site. These are considerations for even the smallest planning project.

Community Planner with a Heart

Wilma recalls about her graduate studies that "most people were either architects or engineers. The architects I could relate to, but the engineers were [very technical] thinkers. I mean, these guys did not consider human beings in their thinking. It was an interesting process. But very cold." This experience taught Wilma something that would stay with her for years to come. She realized that the "human side" of planning was just as important as the technical side. From that time on, Wilma was always sure to think about the people who would live in the communities she designed.

Wilma had always been concerned with social problems in her hometown. Involvement in the region was a Mankiller family tradition. "My father was involved in community work, and our family volunteered in the community," Wilma remembers.

Perhaps that is why Wilma soon turned her efforts to community planning and development for the Cherokee Nation. When she began, her office had no formal program for these efforts. Yet that work had always been Wilma's strongest interest. So she took matters into her own hands and she began to develop social programs. She started with housing and water. Wilma had identified these as the two biggest problems in the region. Later, under the direction of Chief Ross Swimmer, Wilma started to organize the Department of Community Development. She put it together, staffed it, and directed it. Gwen Lemaster, who presently heads the department, recalls Wilma in the early days: "She had a genuine respect for all people. . . . She's loyal to the tribe and she's a loyal friend. But her best tool was hard work, working alongside everyone else. She just worked."

Wilma wanted Cherokee communities to finally get help from someone who understood what it was like to live there. Wilma knew what the top priorities for the region were. And she had the skills to get projects done. It was clear to all who saw Wilma work in those early days that the Cherokee Nation would never be the same again.

". . . Her best tool was hard work, working alongside everyone else."

Chapter 4

The Gifts of
Water and Pride

Even though Wilma's work involved building with concrete and steel, there was another, more human, aspect to her job. Before any projects could begin, Wilma had to convince people in the communities that they could actually help themselves. Simply providing them with houses and water was not enough. They had to learn to trust their own thinking enough to believe they could improve their own lives. As Wilma saw it, the biggest problem in these communities was not housing and water, it was "people's idea that they were in a situation they couldn't do anything about. The single most important part of my work was trying to get people to maintain a sense of hope... and to see that they could come together and actually, physically change their community. They needed to see that they had some control over their own problems."

At the same time, Wilma was challenged with controlling problems of her own. Early in 1980, Wilma fought another battle with death. It was then that she learned she had myasthenia gravis, a disorder of the nervous system. After years of medical treatment and a fierce refusal to be beaten, her disorder went away. Wilma often speaks of the Cherokee "good mind" approach. This approach teaches that painful experiences can often change people for the better. Wilma says that recovering from her disease made her "more focused" and helped her "as a human being." Wilma is best known for that positive attitude.

The Bell Project

In the early 1980s, the community of Bell, near Stilwell, was small and very isolated. About 110 Cherokee families lived there, most of them poor. More than 25 percent of them had no indoor plumbing, and half of them were without a decent income or home. Some people still hunted for the food they ate. The average elderly resident was living on little more than $1,500 a year. And, as in most troubled communities in America, many problems in Bell were settled with violence. Despite all these troubles, Wilma saw many hopeful signs in

Bell. She saw that the residents retained their language and that they depended a great deal on each other. Though most people were poor, they were willing to share what they had with each other. "I thought they were a very tenacious [determined] people," Wilma remembers. "They knew people considered their community a rough place. And they sort of turned inward. They helped each other out. It was that sense of interdependence and tenacity that I built on." And build on it she did—literally.

❖

"It was [a] sense of interdependence that I built on."

Wilma and her future husband, Charlie Soap, supervised the Bell project together. Eventually their efforts brought water to the entire community. By banding the residents together, Wilma organized a work force of incredible power. Together, Wilma and the people of Bell built a 16-mile water pipeline that brought precious water to the area for farming, indoor plumbing, and other important uses.

The Bell project was a success for many reasons. It taught people that they did, indeed, have the power to change their own lives. It showed them that if they worked together, they could complete something as large and complex as a water pipeline. The completion of the project filled everyone involved with great pride. "We all watched our communities change so much," Gwen Lemaster remembers. "We used to be angry and upset—overwhelmed by social problems. But, through Wilma's organizational skills and great personal commitment, we were all able to realize better lives."

One of the proudest participants in the Bell project was Wilma herself. The project proved to Wilma what she had actually known all along. It showed that there was an incredible potential locked inside the people of troubled Cherokee communities. Wilma knew that if poor people are given the resources and a chance—if they are guided by someone who understands their problems—they can be successful. It was Wilma and Charlie Soap who guided them to success.

The Bell water project provided Wilma with some valuable experience. It enabled her to take charge of an important project and to work closely with many different people. It also allowed her to claim some responsibility for Bell's success. These were all things that would serve her well as she entered a new phase in her career. Soon, Wilma Mankiller would be entering tribal politics.

Chapter 5

The First Campaign

Wilma did not think of running for political office as her next logical step. In fact, it took a good deal of convincing from a number of people and, as she says, "a lot of reflection." Wilma recognized that becoming a public figure would be a much different job from the one she had. "It meant making a transition from someone who is purely in a helping and enabling role to someone who has to go out and market herself. That is quite a transition," Wilma recalls.

Quiet and often serious, Wilma also had to decide whether she could be happy "selling herself." Shaking hands, making public speeches, and promoting her ideas openly were all necessary parts of winning an office. But Wilma was a bit uncomfortable with those demands. Still, the idea of "getting into a position where I could make decisions about development and the things I believed in without having to ask somebody else about it" was attractive to her. "All my adult life," Wilma remembers, "I had to go to people in positions of authority. People who had access to resources. I would have to talk them into supporting a new clinic or some new youth or housing project. So the attraction for me was to be able to be in a decision-making position. That way I could just decide 'let's go to Bell, or somewhere else.'"

In the end, the opportunities provided by political office were too good for Wilma to pass up. When Ross Swimmer announced his candidacy for chief of the Cherokee Nation in 1983, he also announced that his running mate was going to be Wilma Mankiller. She would run for the post of deputy chief.

Ross Swimmer was chief of the Cherokee Nation before Wilma.

An Extra Battle

The new candidate was eager to debate the issues with her opponents. And she was determined to work hard for her election. Wilma began campaigning throughout the region. But fellow Cherokees were not greeting her with open arms. And their disapproval was not of her stand on the issues. Nor was it of her running mate. The problem they had was with Wilma's gender.

In 1971, W.W. Keeler became the first Cherokee chief after the nation was granted statehood.

They clearly didn't want a woman running for office.

Wilma was stunned. When she began the campaign, she never thought that she would be dismissed because she was a woman. But a few weeks on the campaign trail made Cherokee disapproval only too obvious. "I hadn't realized that this would happen," Wilma recalls. "It honestly never occurred to me. The work I was doing before, as the community development director, was more usually considered 'male work.' I mean, I had built houses, I put in water systems, I knew heavy equipment. I had supervised carpenters and engineers, and I knew how a backhoe operated. And no one ever said 'you can't do that because you're a woman.' And yet, when I wanted to move to a leadership position, all of a sudden people said 'you can't do that because you're a woman.' It was quite a shock to me."

It took Wilma a while to realize just how serious the issue was. And things soon got worse. One day, Wilma found her car tires had been slashed. People tried three times to burn down a big billboard with Wilma's picture on it. She received countless threatening phone calls. And people personally told Wilma to "get out of the Cherokee race" if she knew what was good for her. One day, a message with pieced-together letters (like a ransom note) also threatened her life.

Despite the hostility in the community, Wilma remained determined. William Ragsdale, assistant to the chief, has said that Wilma's character was able to "surpass the bias" she faced for being a woman. Ragsdale says, "In fact, she was able to overcome it. Someone without that character might not have been able to do that." Throughout that difficult campaign, Wilma's running mate, Ross Swimmer, was supportive and helpful. He helped to keep Wilma's spirit together during the contest. As the campaign went on, Wilma developed techniques to deal with the negative attitudes she faced.

"I decided my being female was a non-issue and that I wasn't going to debate a non-issue," Wilma recalls. "I had ideas about the future of the tribe and I had skills I could bring to the job, so I just stuck to those issues and focused only on that. I think that focus motivated me to campaign a lot harder than I would have otherwise."

Wilma's hard work paid off. By the time voters went to the polls, Wilma had convinced enough of them that she was, in

"There was something quietly intense and determined about [Wilma]."

Wilma greets supporters with John A. Ketcher, deputy chief, on her right.

fact, much more qualified than any of her opponents. The Swimmer/Mankiller ticket was victorious.

Deputy Chief

As deputy chief, Wilma was a high-ranking official in the Cherokee Nation. But she was still only second-in-command. Though her victory in the election focused much attention on her, she was still not able to direct the nation's affairs in the ways she wished. Nevertheless, Wilma's first two years gave her valuable experience. They taught her about politics, power, and how to get things done.

In 1984, after her first year as deputy principal chief, Wilma assumed another role. She became a grandmother when her daughter Felicia gave birth to grandson Aaron Swake.

The next year would bring yet another major change. In 1985, Ross Swimmer received a job offer with the Bureau of Indian Affairs in Washington, D.C. When he accepted, Wilma became the principal chief of the Cherokee Nation. Finally, Wilma Mankiller was at the top.

As an innovative and effective leader, Wilma distinguished herself from the first days she took the office. Lynn Howard, the communications director for the Cherokee Nation, remembers how Wilma was seen by those around her: "In some ways, she defied the stereotypical things you might expect from a leader. She didn't glad-hand. She was just an incredibly strong woman. There was something quietly intense and determined about her."

As the first woman chief in Cherokee history, Wilma got a lot of media coverage. Newspaper and magazine articles praised her efforts. And the attention she got gave her a chance to send her message about the Cherokee Nation to the rest of the world. Just by becoming chief, Wilma had done a great deal to improve the image of Native Americans. When non-Indians saw Wilma and heard her speak, many realized that their ideas about what Indians look and sound like were totally wrong. In addition, Wilma informed people that Indians are not helpless and hostile people who drink too much and hate America. Her message, and the things she did, showed white Americans that Indians have valuable lessons to teach about cooperation, self-reliance, and maintaining a respect for the environment.

Wilma and her husband, Charlie Soap, have worked together on many community projects.

Three years into her post as chief, Wilma's life began to change more rapidly. In 1986, she married for a second time. Her new husband was Charlie Soap. Charlie was a fellow Cherokee who shared Wilma's strong dedication to solving social problems and improving communities. That same year, Wilma's unique work was recognized by a number of distinguished organizations. She was elected to the Oklahoma Woman's Hall of Fame and was also elected American Indian Woman of the Year. She also received an honorary doctorate from the University of New England. Then she received a citation for her outstanding contribution to American leadership from Harvard University.

In 1987, Wilma was up for re-election. Though the work she had done so far had been undeniably successful, the race would not be a sure thing. She faced three strong opponents who ran very tough campaigns. Even the second time, Wilma's being female would be an issue. But this time, she would know much better how to deal with these sexist attitudes.

Chapter 6

Continuing the Job

All in all, Wilma's re-election was much easier than her first campaign. She still had to convince a number of people that a woman could run the Cherokee government. But this time, she had a much stronger record to show for her efforts. Wilma had organized many projects in the area. She had led programs that built health clinics, supported small businesses, and improved the lives of Cherokees throughout the nation. And she showed great skill in managing and motivating people.

Wilma ran against very well-qualified male opponents during her second campaign. Again, she knew that she had to keep them to the real issues. And these issues were not whether a woman could do the job or not. That had already been proven.

The Cherokee people rewarded Wilma with a strong victory in 1987. Her mandate to continue in the role of principal chief was an expression of thanks for the job she had already done. And it was an acknowledgment that her talents were still needed to do even more for the Cherokees in the future.

A Special Kind of Leadership

The Cherokees knew that Wilma was more than just a leader who had brought technology to poor communities. Her leadership meant more to her people than just water lines and electricity. Wilma showed them how to improve their way of life by improving the way they thought of themselves. "The biggest challenge is to get people to have more confidence in their lives," Wilma explains. "The big job here is getting our people to look at their own history, communities, and their own lives for solutions to problems. They need to get out of a way of thinking that says somebody else is going to solve the problems." Wilma believes that much of this way of thinking is due to the brutal treatment of Native Americans throughout the history of the United States. She knows that for a long time, Indians have been made to feel helpless by the U.S. government. For years, the

(Opposite page)
Wilma visits with U.S. Senator Daniel Inouye, chairman of the Senate Select Committee on Indian Affairs.

"The biggest challenge is to get people to have more confidence in their lives."

BIA tried to "mainstream" native peoples. They tried to abolish their governments and forbid the teaching of their language and culture. This treatment has made many Native Americans unable to think of themselves positively. It has weakened their belief that they can actually change things themselves. "Indians are a people," Wilma explains, "who have had their history and culture questioned—in fact their very humanity questioned—for a couple of hundred years. They don't necessarily have the confidence in their own thinking that's required to have a clear vision of their future."

As the tribal leader, Wilma has been able to teach the value of self-reliance to many of her people. And she has set a clear example for all of them by showing, with her own two hands, how the work can get done. "I keep hearing people who sit around saying 'well, *they* are going to solve this problem' but I don't know who *they* are. So I've been trying to tell people that there isn't any *they*. There is only *us*. And a lot of historical things played a part in our being in the situation we are in today. But there is nobody who is going to help dig us out except ourselves. And I think that's the big message for everyone."

Educating the Rest of the World

Not all of Wilma Mankiller's job is done in Oklahoma. In fact, a great part of it is done around the world. To improve the lives of Native Americans, Wilma must teach others about Indian life, culture, and problems. If white people understand the lives and history of the Cherokees, there will be greater willingness to help them to help themselves. And that will be the greatest improvement possible. The way others think of Native Americans affects the way they think of themselves.

Wilma feels the biggest problem to overcome in speaking with others is the lack of knowledge about Native Americans. This lack of understanding causes many people to have false ideas about Indians. Many

A local newscast allows Wilma an opportunity to speak about Native American issues.

As chief, Wilma works
hard to maintain close
personal contact with her
community.

people who don't know better think Wilma
rides to work each day on a horse. In fact,
she uses a station wagon. Many who come
to interview her assume Wilma lives in a
tepee. In fact, she lives in a typical frame
house. Many photographers have asked
her to put on a headdress for photographs.
Wilma prefers to be photographed in her
usual outfit: a business dress.

"I think there's still an incredible amount
of ignorance out there," Wilma explains.
"There's such a lack of accurate information about Cherokee and Indian life. What
happens is people fill in the gaps with
stereotypes. I don't think it's particularly
the fault of most people. They don't know
much about true American history. A lot of
people just have this one mental snapshot
of Indian people, how they lived 300 years

ago. And that's the image they want to keep. Either that or they have a contemporary snapshot of a very troubled, very poor community where basically everything is in decline. Overcoming these stereotypes is the battle."

To fight her battle, Wilma has worked hard to "get the word out." She has given many interviews to newspapers and magazines and has spoken to audiences across the country. In 1987, Wilma received much attention from the national media. She was elected Newsmaker of the Year by Women in Communications, Inc. She was also voted one of the Women of the Year by *Ms.* magazine. And she was featured in *Newsweek* magazine's special edition titled "Celebration of Heroes."

In each place and in each interview, Wilma's message was basically the same: Native Americans are not poor, helpless victims. They are members of a distinct culture that has tremendous courage, determination, and leadership skills. They can improve their situation if they are given the proper chance. It is important to Wilma that the world realizes that. It is also important to her that people not think of Indians as hopeless victims and unproductive members of society.

❖

"I think there's still an incredible amount of ignorance out there . . . about Cherokee and Indian life."

Hollywood's "Indians"

Movies about cowboys and Indians have always been popular in America. During the 1950s and 1960s in particular, many "westerns" were made in Hollywood. These movies most often told stories of pioneers who lived in the unsettled American West. The pioneers would often have to fight various Indians in order to survive. In almost all these movies, the Indians were portrayed as the "bad guys." No one would ever show how the Indians were treated unfairly by the whites. Most of the time, Indians were shown as uncivilized, bloodthirsty, and silly. They often seemed to attack without reason. These portrayals were very unfair.

The people who made these movies in Hollywood knew almost nothing of real Native American culture. They did not really care

Suzan Ball and Victor Mature in a scene from *Chief Crazy Horse,* made in 1955.

Dances With Wolves **tried to show Native Americans as they really were in the 1800s.**

about being accurate. They showed Indians as their audiences wanted to see them. Most movies did not even use real Native American actors to play Indians. Most Indians in movies were played by whites!

Times changed a little during the 1970s and 1980s. More people learned about real Native American culture. Today, Indian characters like those from 1950 would not be accepted. In 1991, a movie called *Dances With Wolves* won an Academy Award for Best Picture. This movie tried to show Native Americans as they really were during the pioneer days. In the movie, real Indians played the characters. And they spoke a real Indian language. This was just one film that tried hard to change the old Hollywood image of Native Americans.

Chapter 7

Looking Back and Looking Forward

Wilma Mankiller has many things to be proud of. When she is asked about what she considers her greatest accomplishments so far, she doesn't think too long. There have been two. First, she is proud of being elected the first woman chief of the Cherokee Nation. For women in her community—and indeed all over the world—Wilma is a shining example of what can be accomplished with intelligence and determination.

Wilma is also proud of her work in community development. Perhaps her most rewarding effort in that field was the Bell project. Wilma got great satisfaction from completing that water pipeline. Looking back, she can see that it accomplished two major things. First, it brought water to a community that had none. Second, it brought members of the community together for a common goal. It showed them the potential they had to change their lives.

Wilma took a chance on the residents of Bell. She saw something in them that she believed in. And she gambled a great deal of money and her reputation on the hope that the project would be a success. "It was a tremendous roll of the dice," Wilma remembers, "and when it actually worked, it affirmed a long-held belief that I've had about my own people—and about poor people in general. I have always felt that poor people have a much greater capacity for leadership and for solving their own problems than anyone has ever given them credit for." Once the Bell water system was complete, Wilma could see that her instincts had guided her correctly. Bell would never be the same again. And neither would Wilma Mankiller.

Wilma recovers after a kidney transplant in a Massachusetts hospital, July, 1990. Her new kidney was donated by her brother.

Facing Today's Challenges

Although she underwent a kidney transplant in July of 1990, Wilma did not let her operation slow her down. Her recovery was remarkably quick. And her determination to return at full power was never shaken. In a matter of a few weeks, Wilma was back at her desk, ready to work.

Today, Wilma continues to improve Cherokee life in a number of ways. She and other members of her administration

are in the process of reworking the tribal judicial system. The Cherokees have their own laws that are independent of the U.S. federal or state governments. Much of the old and complex tribal judicial system has disappeared since the turn of the century. But now new concerns over land disputes and commercial development make it necessary for the Cherokees to bring their systems of justice back to life.

In addition, the Cherokees have recently established a new tax commission. That commission will explore the possibility of taxing businesses on tribal lands. This will

Wilma says she doesn't want to become too "removed from people" as chief because it's the people that inspire her to keep working.

Wilma sits at her desk in October of 1990.

create much-needed revenue for the Cherokee Nation. It will also help them to become less dependent on outside sources for funding.

A new agreement with the federal government, signed in 1990, will give Wilma and her administration even more independence. The Tribal Self-Governance Agreement takes control of the Cherokee budget away from the federal government and puts it in the hands of the Cherokees themselves. Now that Wilma is in control of the money she spends, she feels able to create and fund programs faster. And this makes her ideas more effective.

What the Future Holds

Many people ask Wilma if she will seek a larger political office. The answer is a firm "no." "I'm not interested at all in mainstream political office for myself," Wilma explains. "I am more interested in working for other women and other Indians. I like building clinics. I like building houses. I like doing things you can reach out and touch. People in political offices are often too removed from the people. You don't get to meet and interact with them. And that's what I like to do."

Before the June election in 1991, many people asked Wilma if she would run again. Her answer at that time was, "I've been here for almost 14 years now and it becomes more and more difficult to dedicate another four-year block of time. It's a big commitment. Now would be a good time to do something else." But, as the election came closer, Wilma began to change her mind. Finally, just a few months before the campaign got underway, Wilma announced her decision: she would run again.

Even though Wilma has many other interests and goals she has yet to accomplish, her heart will always remain with the Cherokee Nation. It is there that she has

❖

"I like doing things you can reach out and touch."

accomplished her greatest tasks. And it is there that she feels the most comfortable and useful.

As a leader, Wilma has accomplished many things. She has brought the basic necessities of life to many poor and struggling families. But she has also paved an easier way for future Indian leaders. As Assistant to the Chief William Ragsdale has

The Cherokee National Museum in Tahlequah houses a large collection of exhibits on Native American culture and Cherokee history.

said, "Wilma has gone beyond the 'buck-skin curtain.' She has taken some of the mysticism away from being a tribal chief. She's demonstrated that a chief is not some mythical kind of creature. She doesn't try to show that our government is perfect. But she has been able to project a *real* Indian character to the world. And she has been able to find acceptance for us in the family of American government."

William Ragsdale is not the only one who appreciates Wilma's special kind of leadership. On June 15, 1991, Wilma was elected to her second full term as chief. This time she got 83 percent of the vote! Wilma's landslide victory was a clear vote of confidence in her abilities. On August 14, 1991, Wilma officially began her second four-year term.

The future for the Cherokees and for Wilma still holds many challenges. Many problems remain to be solved. But, no matter what the future holds, it is certain that Chief Mankiller will continue to guide the Cherokee Nation—indeed, all Native Americans—down a road of continued progress and hope for a better life.

Glossary
Explaining New Words

ancestor A family relative from generations long ago.

clan A group of families descending from a common ancestor.

community Any group, living in the same area, sharing common lifestyles, interests, or work.

culture The skills, arts, and traditions of a people.

ethnic A group of people that share a similar culture.

gender Sex; male or female.

heritage Traditions passed down from generation to generation.

ignorance A lack of knowledge or understanding.

Native Americans The earliest settlers of North America, also known as Indians.

Sequoya Developed the Cherokee alphabet, making a strong written tradition possible.

stereotype An exaggerated idea about a race or culture of people.

tribe A group of persons or clans that share common ancestors and are governed by a leader, or chief.

For Further Reading

Josephy, Alvin. *History of the Native Americans.* Six Volumes. Morristown: Silver Burdett Press, 1990.

Lepthien, E. *The Cherokee.* Chicago: Childrens Press, 1990.

Mancini, Richard E. *Indians of the Southeast.* New York: Facts On File, 1991.

Porter, Dr. Frank W. *The Cherokee.* Broomall, Pennsylvania: Chelsea House Publishers, 1990.

Voices From Our Country, Sourcebook Series. Austin: Steck-Vaughn Publishers, 1990.

Index

Photo credits:
Cover, pages 1, 4: ©Tom Gilbert; p. 6, 40, 57, 59: Bruce Glassman; p. 8, 30, 38, 47, 50, 56:
©Dan Agent/Cherokee Nation; p. 9, 23, 34, 42, 44, 45, 49, 54, 55: courtesy Cherokee Nation;
p. 12, 13, 14, 15: North Wind; p. 16: Private Collection; p. 20–21: "The Trail of Tears," by
Robert Lindneaux/Woolaroc Museum, Bartlesville, OK; p. 22, 39: The Bettmann Archive;
p. 24, 25: courtesy Museum of the American Indian, New York, NY; p. 29: courtesy San
Francisco State University, Office of Public Affairs; p. 31: University of Arkansas, Special
Collections Department.

Photo Research by **Inge King.**

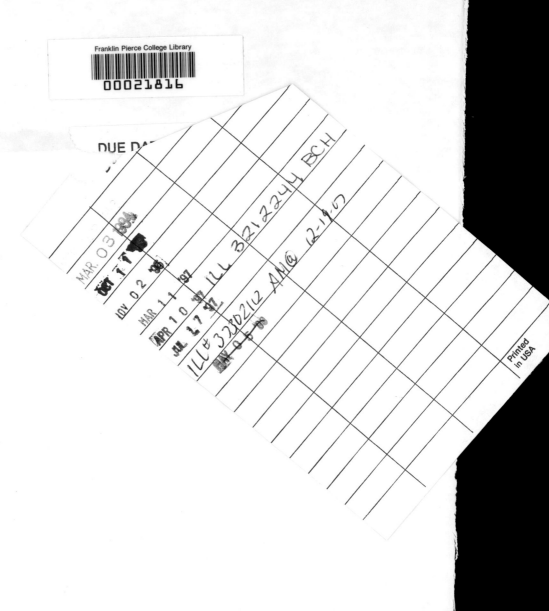